Old Soul, Young Spirit

Also by Adolfo Quezada

Compassionate Awareness
Radical Love
Sabbath Moments
Loving yourself for God's Sake
Wholeness: The Legacy of Jesus
Walking with God
Goodbye My Son, Hello
Rising from the Ashes
A Desert Place
Heart Peace
Of Mind and Spirit
Through the Darkness

The Teachings of Jesus
Interpreted for Everyday Living

Transcending Illness
through the Power of Belief

For John & Lorraine,

With love,

Adolfo

Old Soul, Young Spirit

Reflections on Growing Old

Adolfo Quezada

CONTENTS

Part Four

Part Five

Part Six

Part Seven

Part Eight

*To Irma, Fernando, and Yolanda,
my siblings and fellow-travelers on
this adventurous journey of old age.*

Foreword

It's not easy growing old in America. After all, we invented the cult of youth and beauty. At least Hollywood did along with scary movies, Fast and Furious and happy endings. So if one happens to be old and ugly, slow and irascible, one tends to be looked upon with a modicum of distain.

The local Barnes and Noble bookstore has two wide shelves of books devoted to aging. Some are about coping with aging parents and the ravages of Alzheimer's. There is one titled "Younger Next Year," aimed at women and apparently contradicting the notion another year makes you older. There is also a book called "Paleo," having to do with ancient diets. Yet another age-defying title is "Superfit: The 5 Forces That Will Make You Healthy, Fit and Eternally Awesome." It seems that "eternally awesome" is a bit of a stretch unless you refer to the Grand Canyon. This one is intriguing: "What Makes Olga Run? The Mystery of the 90-something Track Star." Even

Martha Stewart has a book, "Living the Good Long Life."

It's likely Barnes and Noble will be expanding its section on aging. The market is growing. Between 2000 and 2010, the over 65 crowd grew faster than the rest of the population. By 2013, the U.S. Census Bureau estimated that 44.7 million Americans were 65 or over, comprising 14.5 % of the total population.

The 2010 census showed a 30.4 percent growth rate among 65 to 69 year olds, from 9.5 million to 12.4 million. And naturally, there's more to come.

The most surprising group of all was the 85 to 94 year olds, which grew at the extraordinary rate of nearly 30 percent. That group's numbers increased from 3.9 million to 5.1 million.

The increase in books on aging will also spur an increase in prescriptive advice, primarily focusing on preservation of youth, which everyone knows is wasted on the young. Most of these books will tell you what to do, how to do it and why. It is worth some consideration and cogitation on the reasons the species is genetically disposed to dictate how others should act and think, what to do and when to do it. It is a tiresome business, and some become caught up in the need to control and manipulate others. You may have encountered one or two of them in what New Agers like to call your Life Journey.

I still remember a New Yorker cartoon that shows a man reading the obituary pages. Two pages are spread out with the back of the man's head in the middle and thought bubbles strewn across the drawing. The bubbles contain one of two possible thoughts: "Younger than me" and "Older than me." It's what we do. We're human. There are no certainties and a whole lot to be nervous about. There are a lot more mysteries than Olga the track star. Life's journey doesn't require a lot of close examination if you are fortunate like most of us and not in need of psychotherapy.

But old age imposes limitations, infirmities and greater proximity to mortality. That's when the complaints begin. The pace slows, the back hurts, joints ache and, Lord knows, it takes twice as long to open a package. Chances are you have been offered this advice by an old person: "Don't get old." It is not possible but such advice is more than that. It's the wrong approach, the wrong way of seeing old age. Mark Twain had it right: "Do not complain about growing old. It's a privilege denied to many."

This book *Old Soul, Young Spirit: Reflections on Growing Old* adopts a similarly optimistic view on aging. It does not prescribe. It provides no magic nostrums for eternal youth. Instead, its author Adolfo Quezada, a counselor of many years, centers on the soul and the spirit. If there is any instruction in *Old Soul, Young Spirit*, it is in helping you to explore a path to contentment in aging. It does this by describing ideals, the best way to think about such vital matters as loss, fear, uncertainty, one's purpose, death, and, of course, love.

There are references to God in this book, but it is not strictly speaking a religious book. It assumes a strong faith and often suggests prayer and meditation in relation to God. But an atheist and the secular humanist will discover much in the ideals Quezada describes.

This is a short book, but it is long on thought. It is a book to be kept close by after the first reading because ideals have a way of slipping out of mind. This is a book that offers a balance to aging that I dare say you won't find on those shelves at Barnes and Noble. At least not until this one is placed there.

Steve Auslander
Former Editor
Arizona Daily Star

Preface

We have been born into a new life that we call "old age."

We accept this stage of our life not only as inevitable, but as an integral part of our life experience. And even as we prepare to traverse the sometimes rough terrain of aging, our aim is not to simply endure the rugged journey, but to grow old consciously, courageously, and contentedly.

While it is not within our power to stop ourselves from growing old, it is within our power to grow old healthily by taking good care of our body, mind, and spirit.

Growing old is more than just aging. Aging is what happens to our mind and body with the passing of time; *growing* old is what happens to us spiritually as we stay attentive to our moments and remain wide awake through this chapter of our life.

The Greek playwright Aristophanes once commented that the old are in a second childhood. It is not clear whether he meant that those in their later years are helpless and vulnerable like children; or that they are simple, wonder-filled, and humble of heart like children. In any case, it is true that as we get older we crave simplicity and hunger for authenticity.

Old age takes us out from behind the masks we used to wear, and deprives us of the roles we used to play. As we grow old we seem to have less and less tolerance for the superficial. Life is too short, especially now, for falsity and pretense. By now we have been through too much to accept anything short of the truth.

Old souls are like young souls; both are ready to experience life with an open mind and a courageous heart.

Old age is our last chance to live out the life we have always wanted to live. This does not mean that when we turn 75 years old we will join the circus or that when we reach 85 years of age we will become a forest ranger. We are all impressed by news reports that feature remarkable men and women who swim the English Channel in their 60s, and those who skydive in their 90s. These stories are interesting and inspiring, but they are not examples of what we aspire to. While we can be impressed by extraordinary feats, we generally accept ourselves just as we are, limitations and all; and we don't compare ourselves with others. Neither do we judge ourselves according to how others perform. We figure that it is remarkable enough for us just to have gotten to this point in our life.

We are not old people trying to be young; we are old people whose youth is still a part of us, as is all of our previous life experience. As we grow old we may forget details about our past, but our youthful nature was etched into our memory and will be part of us until the day we die.

We are growing old, but our experience with old age is brand new. In old age we begin to see the world through a more forgiving lens, and to experience life with a more open heart.

We have all heard the jokes that stereotype old people as tired geezers, prone to falling asleep in theaters, family gatherings, and even on the floor of Congress. Actually, old age is the time when many of us begin to awaken to the realizations that we slept through in our youth.

As we grow old we awaken to the transitory nature of our earthly life and the eternal nature of our soul. We awaken to the putrefying consequences of living with resentments and the liberating effects of forgiveness. We awaken to our life's season of winter: a time to slow down, become quiet, and die back so that new growth may come forth. We awaken to the moment before us and to our responsibility to live it fully. And we awaken to God-consciousness, and to the basic needs of others.

Our body deteriorates faster as we grow old, and we look less and less attractive. This is plain to see. What is not so clearly seen is the part of us that never grows old and never dies – our soul.

Our soul, the essence of who we are, the core of our being, is timeless, changeless, and ageless. It regenerates our life even in old age. Though we may move a little slower and reminisce a little longer, the spirit animates our soul, and we are imbued with hope and vitality.

Staying as physically healthy as we can is definitely a priority for us; as is remaining mentally viable, and spiritually alive. But it is not our intent to do battle with old age. Instead, we embrace this special time in our life, and enter into it wholeheartedly.

Old age is not quitting time; but neither is it a time for acceleration. Rather, it is a time to gather ourselves as we prepare for the end of our life. It is a time to complete unfinished business, reconcile estrangements where appropriate, and enter into deeper communion with God.

We are no longer reaching for the stars of fame, fortune, and power; but there is nothing stopping us from reaching for the stars of wisdom, equanimity, and contentment.

We may be old and somewhat incapacitated; and we may even seem useless to some; but in the depths of our being abides the spirit of love that retrieves us from the brink of insignificance, invigorates our soul, and awakens our heart to serve others in the name of God.

Part One
Growing Old

For age is opportunity no less
than youth itself, though in another dress,
and as the evening twilight fades away,
the sky is filled with stars, invisible by day.
Henry Wadsworth Longfellow

Surrendering Youth

Take kindly the counsel of the years,
gracefully surrendering the things of youth.
Desiderata

In our youth we prided ourselves on our prowess.

If there was a mountain to climb, literally or figuratively, we were ready to do it. We learned the lessons and obtained the skills to take on nearly impossible work. We believed that nothing was insurmountable for us. We climbed and climbed our way to the top; performance was what mattered; success was our main goal.

In our old age we behold the mountain in awe and wonderment, but we stay in the valley in comfort and repose. No longer do we need to prove ourselves; no longer must we strive. We remember well the mountaintop, and the memories are sweet; yet today the valley calls us to a plain and simple life. We walk through the valley of the shadow of death; we walk through the valley of hope.

In our youth we were creative. We dreamed dreams and worked to realize them. We unfettered our imagination and followed its lead. We invented the improbable, and beautified our world with our creations.

In our old age we are open to receive all that life bestows on us. We are grateful for the generosity of others; we accept our limitations; we enjoy the gifts of nature; and we anticipate our time of death.

In our youth we set high goals and worked hard to achieve them. Sometimes we worked through our lunch break and sometimes we worked extra hours to get the job done. We spared nothing in our effort to complete our commitments. Sometimes our health was affected; sometimes our family took the brunt of our sacrifice.

Growing old, whether retired or not, we have learned to live in moderation. We work moderately, we play moderately, we are moderate in our commitments, and, above all, we are not afraid to stop and rest from time to time.

In our youth we moved to get things done. We moved to get from one place to another, we moved to keep up with the others, and we moved to avoid stagnation. In our old age we dare to be still. We are still to pray and meditate, we are still to let our soul catch up with us, we are still to listen to the hummingbird, and we are still to know that God is God.

As we transitioned from youth to old age, a lot of things transitioned with us. We became less ego-centric and more concerned with the well-being of others. We cut back on *doing* and are more about *being*. We are still willing to receive from others, yet we are prepared to give of ourselves and of our treasure, time, and talent.

When we were young we gave ourselves much importance. Years of experience have taught us that, although we are indeed important in the eyes of God, we need to let go of self-aggrandizement because, rather than attract others, it repulses them. It is better for us to walk in humility among our fellow beings than to float above them and out of reach.

We are forced to let go of many things as we grow old, but there are some things that we voluntarily let go of as we mature. We have learned, for example, to let go of our illusion of control over the lives of others. We have learned, sometimes the hard way, that we only have control over our own life, and sometimes not even that.

Our busy life in our younger years forced us to multitask. We didn't mind, in fact, it stimulated us and got our adrenalin going. Doing several things at the same time was actually praised and rewarded. To be exhausted at the end of the day was a badge of honor. But growing old is hard enough without having to do more than one thing at a time. Old age is a time to give the task before us our undivided attention.

As we grow old we realize that we are not needed in the same way as we were before. Others do not count on us as they used to in our younger years. Because being needed motivated us in the past, not being needed as much is a major adjustment for us; and we grieve that loss. The adjustment we make is that, while we are not needed in the same ways as before, we look for ways in which we are still needed – sometimes they are ways that only someone in old age can respond to.

Transition

This journey then, is nothing more, yet nothing less than a period of acclimating to a new way of seeing, a time of transition and revelation as it gradually comes upon "that" which remains when there is no self.

Bernadette Roberts

As we grow old our attention begins to shift toward the more essential aspects of life.

While in our younger years we may have focused much of our attention on advancing our career or making a major contribution to the world; in our older years we are more likely to give our attention to staying healthy. If we were more concerned about being liked and accepted by others before, in our old age we are not about fulfilling the expectations that others may have of us. We now place more importance on self-acceptance.

In our earlier years we let the wind blow us where it willed, but in our later years it has served us well to add structure to our life. This does not mean that we get ourselves into a boring rut that allows for little spontaneity or adventure. Rather, it means that by establishing and committing to a regular routine that includes a time to meditate, pray, work, play, exercise, and learn we enhance our quality of life.

We will never be as spontaneous and impulsive as we were in our youth, but an unexpected adventure now and then turns monotony into joy.

In our youth we pushed for change. We wanted to try new things and allow for innovation. We wanted to update the old and modernize our world. We wanted to discard the stale and the antiquated, and to introduce the latest trend.

In our old age we hold out for our tradition. Keeping with tradition, we know what we can count on, we honor where we come from, we find comfort in what's familiar, and we pass on what we have known to those who come after us.

In our younger years we played many roles, depending on our circumstances, obligations, aspirations, or the image we wanted to present to the world. Some roles were personal, others were professional, yet others we played in order to get what we wanted. But whether they helped us or not, none of these roles depicted our true self. In our old age we dare to stop playing roles and instead, reveal to the world our essential self. No more pretending to be who we are not, no more hiding who we are.

In our youth we were inspired by our dreams, motivated by our idealism, and energized by our determination. In our old age, with many battles, causes, and crusades behind us; we have learned that motivation, idealism, and determination are not enough to accomplish our work successfully. We need, above all else, the divine force that animates our soul, and directs our work.

The Fruits of Old Age

In old age they still produce fruit;
they are always green and full of sap…
Ps 92:14

Sweet are the fruits of old age; luscious is its yield. Even as the decades pass, we flourish and contribute.

Fortunately, old age did not take from us the fruit of creativity. Whatever our mode of creative expression, it continues to transform us. Perhaps it is because we have more free time available to us in old age that some of us wait until our later years to launch our creative endeavors. Or maybe it's because we have gathered much material through the years with which to work. It could also be that we have finally given ourselves permission to express ourselves with creative abandon.

Exposing our creative work to the world is usually frightening to us, but old age is a time of confidence, courage, and freedom to be our true selves as revealed through our creativity.

Old age has not taken from us the fruits of curiosity, caring, and compassion. Through the decades of our life we witnessed many atrocities perpetrated against humanity. Yet, years of wars, terrorism, epidemics, and natural disasters have not jaded us. On the contrary, we continue learning about our planet and the people who inhabit it.

We keep abreast of current affairs because we believe that the welfare of our fellow human beings on the other side of the world is just as important as that of our closest neighbor.

Even in our old age we are still in love with life. We partake of the fruit of contented living. Simple pleasures come to us spontaneously and unexpectedly. A sunrise, a sunset, a rainbow, or a cloud; suddenly it is there in brilliant colors and indescribable beauty. A moment of silent solitude, a walk in the park, a heartfelt conversation with a friend, or an hour lost in our creativity: these are the times of our life that feed our soul and sustain us for another day.

Not all the fruits of old age are low hanging; some are harder to come by than others. The fruit of well-being requires us to be disciplined in how we take care of ourselves. The fruit of mental viability compels us to reach higher and higher to learn and ponder what our mind takes in. And the fruit of spiritual awakening invites us to ascend to the highest heights and descend to the deepest depths as we contemplate the nature and purpose of our existence.

Winter Grace

Youth, large, lusty, loving – youth,
full of grace, force, fascination.
Do you know that old age may come
after you with equal grace, force, fascination?
Walt Whitman

We are not as strong in our old age as we were when we were younger; we are not as flexible as before; and we are apt to be more set in our ways than we used to be.

Sometimes we have a hard time with new ideas; and we don't bounce back from injuries or illnesses as quickly as we did in the past.

The good news is that it is not strength or flexibility that we need in old age as much as an ability to absorb the shocks that come with later life. We have learned through our experience to give way to the shocks and unexpected events in the same way that a martial arts warrior rolls with the force of the opponent's attack.

There is a strong character that comes with old age. Swiss psychiatrist Carl Jung referred to it as "winter grace." It enables us to maintain our integrity even in the face of the losses, health problems, and the ominous and ubiquitous threat of death. God graces us with the necessary tools to meet our needs and the needs of others.

Grace is the overwhelming flow of God's unconditional love. It is God's power of healing, illuminating, and reconciling. But grace cannot be possessed. It is free. We cannot control it. Sometimes it comes when we least expect it. It comes in times of turmoil, failure, conflict, boredom, addiction, trouble, and crisis. Grace cannot be stopped. It breaks through in spite of us.

Through the grace of God we come to realize that it is in our powerlessness, our weakness, and our vulnerability that we become open, available, and receptive to the influence of God.

The trust we have developed in old age is not necessarily trust in persons or things. Rather, it is an overall trust in the grace of God, regardless of the circumstances of our life. It is trust in the inviolability of our soul. Within that trust, we venture wholeheartedly into life; we let go of our illusion of control; and we risk surrendering to the unknown. With trust, we allow our mind to be silent and our body to be still. We let go and dare to just be.

Sometimes hope gives way to doubt and we are at loose ends. But doubt does not signify a lack of faith, rather its presence. Only in faith do we dare to venture courageously into the dark unchartered waters of old age without the certainty that we will be all right.

Part Two
Transformation

*Changing is not just changing the things
outside of us. First of all we need the right
view that transcends all notions including of
being and nonbeing, creator and creature,
mind and spirit. That kind of insight is
crucial for transformation and healing.*
Thich Nhat Hanh

Limitations

Very Truly, I tell you, when you were younger, you used to fasten your own belt and go wherever you wished. But when you grow old, you will stretch out your hands, and someone else will fasten a belt around you and take you where you do not wish to go.

Jn 21:18

Old age sneaks up on us. When we least expect it the signs begin to show up.

I was surprised by a young, petite female clerk in the pet store who asked me if I needed her help to carry out a 40-pound bag of dog food to my car. Apparently, she knew I was old before I did. Of course I told her thank you, but no, I could handle it - my back hurt for two weeks. What surprised me even more was that the next time I went to the pet store and she asked me again if I needed help, I said yes.

Just because we feel young on the inside doesn't mean that we are. But getting our inside to catch up with our outside takes a while. Sometimes it is our pride that blinds us to our need for help; sometimes it is simple denial of how old we are getting. Sometimes we decline assistance because we fear appearing weak or admitting vulnerability.

We also tell ourselves that if we accept help we will become obligated to the helper. Another obstacle to our accepting help from others is our need to stay in control. There is even some anticipation that our request for help might be rejected.

It is quite humbling to start seeing ourselves as the old men and women that we are. But eventually, we realize that we have no choice. We can appear self-reliant and independent by carrying the load alone – and perhaps hurt ourselves – or we can accept our limitations and allow others to help us.

Of course it makes sense that we prefer to be strong and self-sufficient; and of course we want to be independent for as long as we can. But when physical or mental limitations bring our life to a standstill; and when deterioration of our body or mind prevent us from doing for ourselves, then, instead of dreading our dependence on others, we can be grateful to them for helping us meet our basic needs.

The older we get, the more limitations we experience, and the more assistance we require. Eventually, we will need help with our personal care, with transportation to medical appointments, and with shopping. If and when we develop serious disabling physical conditions or memory loss, we will need substantial help.

Allowing the love and compassion of others to be helpful to us is worth the risk. By allowing ourselves to be helped we benefit greatly from the kindness and generosity of others, including strangers, who are willing to tend to us.

With every day that passes in our old age it seems we are confronted with a new limitation. It may be something that limits us physically, mentally, or both. Of course, new restrictions imposed on us are frustrating and sometimes depressing. In a way, limitations shrink our world. Each limitation means that there is one more thing that we cannot do or one more place we cannot go. Whether it is a major or a minor loss that we experience, we know that we must take the time to grieve it.

There is a lot about growing old that is tough, yet, for the most part, we are prepared to handle it. But there is one thing we especially fear about growing old, and that is the loss of our independence. Let us hope that we can conjure up the will to let go of the control we have enjoyed for all these years. Let us pray that some measure of humility will overcome the pride in us that keeps us from asking for help. May we have the courage to let go of our illusion of self-sufficiency. May we have the humility to accept what is, and to make the best of it. May we have the faith and foresight to give meaning and purpose to our limitations, and the gratitude to be content with what we have.

Change

All great changes are preceded by chaos.
Deepak Chopra

We may lose flexibility in our spine and joints as we get old, but that doesn't mean that we can't be mentally flexible as we adapt to all the changes that come with the passing of years, including our health. Such flexibility necessitates an open mind, a forgiving heart, and an expansive spirit.

Our life has changed dramatically in old age. It alternates between chaos and order. People close to us have died, our good health that we had counted on has begun to deteriorate, and the technology that we finally understood is now obsolete. Little by little we bring order back to our life. We grieve our loved ones, and adjust to a world without them; we adapt to our physical limitations; and we learn new technology. But we cannot become complacent because chaos is already knocking on our door again. As we grow old we learn that chaos is the matrix of order and order is the matrix of chaos. We learn that without chaos there is no creativity or ingenuity; and without order there is no stability or reliability. Chaos and order are the yin and yang of our existence, the soul and spirit of our life.

Old age has taught us that nothing stays the same. What is today will not be tomorrow, and it will change again the day after tomorrow. We have learned that the very nature of life is change. So, although we may revert to the same daily routines, and we may stick to predictable behaviors that provide us with a sense of comfort, we are clearly aware that what we do is never exactly the same from one time to the next. We know that although we may walk the same path each morning, everything we see along that path and our experience of it, changes from day to day. While we are comforted by what is familiar to us, we do not count on anything to remain unchanged. Instead, we ride the wave of change, but anchor ourselves to the immutable presence of God.

Loss

When the heart weeps for what it has lost,
the soul laughs for what it has found.
                    Sufi aphorism

If old age is nothing else, it is a time of great and small losses.

We begin by losing functionality. Little by little we start noticing deterioration in our ability to see, hear, move, think, and remember. If we have spent our life identifying ourselves with what we do, then our inability to function at full capacity is a major loss.

How ironic that at the time in our life when we are becoming more aware of the world through our senses, our senses are beginning to malfunction. We can gaze at the breath-taking beauty of the winter moon in awe and wonder, but we may have to squint our eyes a little. We can enjoy the sweet music coming from the radio, but we may have to turn up the volume a little. And we can eat our favorite food, anticipating the taste of flavors we've always known and loved, but we may have to spice it up a little.

With every passing decade our health takes a hit. Sometimes we develop serious illnesses, sometimes we become chronically sick. Illness incapacitates us to such an extent that we are forced to change our lifestyle dramatically.

We may develop problems with mobility, which further limits our ability to do for ourselves. In turn, we lose the independence we have enjoyed all of our life.

As we get older we are compelled by poor eyesight and compromised coordination to give up our driver's license. Now we are trapped at home unless we can solicit a ride from someone. We have cherished control over our own life and now we must give it up slowly, but surely.

In our old age we have the curse and the privilege to see our loved ones die. With every death of a friend or family member our heart is broken again. As we grow old we start to notice that many of our friends and relatives with whom we grew up and whom we have known throughout our life are no longer alive. And it seems that with every year that passes there are less of them. These are persons whom we knew and loved, but they are also persons who knew and loved us. They understood where we came from and how it was for us growing up. Now they are no longer here and we feel more and more alone and lonely. As our family and friends, especially our contemporaries, continue to die, we are reminded of our own mortality.

Through a life of losses we have learned the hard way that unless we grieve what we have lost; whether as a result of death, illness, incapacitation, or old age, we will suffer our loss forever. When, however, we take the time to mourn what is no more, we eventually stumble out of the dark night of grief and enter into the light of new life. As we adapt to our loss through grief we realize that our whole world has changed, including us.

Transformed by Loss

O unsupportable and touching loss!
William Shakespeare

Perhaps the greatest personal transformation that occurs after losing a loved one to death is the manner in which we respond to life.

We respond from our grief; that is, from our recognition that we have suffered a tremendous loss and our life will never be the same again.

We feel the full impact of the loss that comes with living and loving; we experience the emotions that manifest the torment within; and we allow the transformation that comes in the wake of loss. In short, we change our way of being.

Before our loss some of us were prone to indolence, and any effort seemed more than we could muster. We tended to procrastinate doing what needed to be done because we figured that there was always tomorrow. But through our death experience we came to realize that our days are numbered; and we are awakened to our more assertive selves. Conscious that death is waiting in the wings, we are motivated to overcome our inertia and take action for the good of all.

Before our loss some of us were mired in anger toward others and what we held against them ensnarled us in a web of negative memories and toxic grudges. But now we realize that life is too short to waste on resentments. We have been moved to forgive those who have injured us and to release them of their debts to us. Our anger decreases as our mercy increases.

When we have been broken by our intimate experience with death, we respond to life from our emptiness. Yet, it is because of our emptiness that we are receptive to the growth that comes in the aftermath of our loss. Our encounter with death changes us dramatically.

Before our loss some of us deceived others to gain their love and acceptance because we were afraid to show them the color of our soul lest we be rejected. We did it by trying to impress them with our achievements and our appearance in hope that they would think that was who we were. We stayed busy and moved with haste because we were afraid that the truth would catch up to us. We tried to hide behind facades, but death saw through our masks. When we were confronted with our mortality, our pretenses fell away because death makes honest persons of us all.

Before our loss some of us failed to appreciate our own life and instead became envious of who others were and what they had. But when our life was threatened by illness, or accident, or old age, we suddenly became more protective of the life we were living.

Now we would not trade our life for anyone else's life. A glimpse of our mortality was enough to prompt us to respect and be grateful for our life just as it is.

Before our loss some of us were gripped by inordinate fear that immobilized our life and desensitized our heart. We were fearful of what could happen to threaten our status quo. We demanded security at any cost, even if it inhibited life itself. We feared death the most because it would take away all that we had. Yet, when we experienced death up close, we were transformed. If death has taken a loved one away from us, there is nothing more that can hurt us now, or so it seems. In the wake of death's blow, we are left bereft, but courageous; devastated, but no longer afraid to die.

Before our loss pride blinded some of us to the reality of our humanity, and we exalted ourselves beyond recognition. Our arrogance separated us from the very ones to whom we wished to be close. But when death came knocking on our neighbor's door, or that of a friend or family member, or perhaps our own door, we descended abruptly to the ground of our being. Death is the ultimate equalizer.

Before our loss some of us were insatiable and believed that we had to take in as much as we could lest we be gone tomorrow. We believed that more is better and we set out to ingest and imbibe all that life had to offer. Our gluttony filled us, but it didn't fulfill us. It kept us from acknowledging the suffering that comes with loving and losing. We didn't want to be drawn into our painful emotions. But death pierced our heart and dragged us deep into our emotions. When we surfaced we were different.

Now it is not enough for us to keep taking more and more; now we must consider our losses too; now we must allow ourselves to experience the ecstasy of love *and* the agony of loss.

Part Three
Vicissitudes

Old age is not a disease – it is strength and survivorship, triumph over all kinds of vicissitudes and disappointments, trials, and illnesses.

                                        Maggie Kuhn

Uncertainty

So even to old age and gray hairs,
O God, do not forsake me.
Ps 71:18

The storms of life keep coming as we grow old; and faith is our response.

It is not a faith that everything will turn out the way we would prefer, but a faith that, no matter what happens, we have been graced with the wherewithal to handle it. Faith is not total fearlessness, but a wholehearted response to life.

We have had a lifetime of uncertainty, so we have no illusions that anything is for sure. But this does not mean that we have stopped making plans or commitments for the future. It means that, while we are prepared to carry out our plans and honor our commitments, we are also perfectly aware that life is fluid and that circumstances change.

We know that sometimes the best laid plans go awry, and the most sincere commitments are sometimes scuttled. The years have tempered our expectations and have removed the element of surprise when things don't go the way we meant for them to go.

It isn't that we have adopted an attitude of doubt and cynicism; rather, we have just become more realistic. Let's just say that we have become proficient at developing contingency plans.

Just because old people cling less and less to absolutes, and instead entertain all kinds of possibilities, doesn't mean that we are confused. On the contrary, it means that we can tolerate the tension of opposites, and can allow for contingencies.

As we grow old we learn that not everything is unequivocal, absolute, or unambiguous; rather, it can also be relative, contingent, and unpredictable. Uncertainty is constant in old age, but when we are conscious of God in our life, we know how best to deal with what comes.

Grounded in our truest nature, we respond to life's uncertainties with creativity, courage, and contentment.

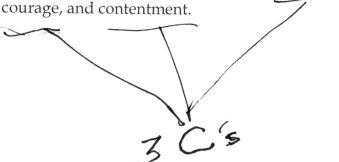

3 C's

Fear

Do not fear, for I am with you, do not be afraid,
for I am your God; I will strengthen you, I will help
you…

Isa 41:10

It is normal for us to fear experiences that are unfamiliar to us. Old age is one of those experiences.

We fear losing our memory, and we fear that illness might be just around the corner. Another major fear we have in old age is that eventually we may become a burden to others.

How do we respond to the cruel reality that old age can sometimes bring? How do we confront the probability of decrepitude? How do we face the certainty of death? We respond to these challenging years not with gritted teeth and dogged determination, but with vulnerability, humility, and faith in the power within us that will see us through the worst of times.

We confront whatever comes not with fear and trepidation, but with the courage of a lioness and the patience of Job. We face our end of life not in anguish and despair, but with peace in our mind and love in our heart. We have learned in our old age that our fears disappear when we turn and confront what threatens us. Our antidote for fear and anxiety is to get grounded in the security of our inner being where God abides.

We do not totally eliminate fear from our emotions because fear helps us to survive. But we don't allow fear to take over our life. It is important that we acknowledge our fear, experience it, and express it.

The courage that sustains us through our fear and enables us to move ahead in spite of our fear comes from our heartfelt belief that we are part of something greater and stronger than our fear. This divine refuge holds our fear, along with our courage, and comforts us through the storm.

The faith that abates our fear is not based on the belief that all will be well, but rather that, no matter what happens, we have what it takes to respond to it with courage and acceptance.

Suffering

The wound is the place where the light enters you.
Rumi

By the time we reach old age we are well acquainted with suffering.

Suffering has been our companion for a long time. As we look back to times of suffering we remember the darkness of it all; yet, we also remember that suffering has brought us light. It has shaken us out of complacency and has awakened us in ways we did not anticipate.

If before we suffered we avoided feeling emotions, suffering has plunged us into the depths of passion and compassion; sympathy and understanding. Because we have known pain, we have learned to empathize with others who are hurting. Because we have felt anger and fear, we have come to understand the humanness of those emotions. Suffering is not to be recommended as a maturation aide; but when it comes – as it surely does – we

51

learn from it, we change from it, and we grow from it.

We have come to accept suffering as a necessary part of growing old. But this does not mean that we seek it out or otherwise welcome it into our life. Only when suffering is truly inevitable do we cease our resistance to it and enter into it with our whole being.

To accept suffering means that we come to terms with it. It does not mean that we become victims of it, but that we face it with resilience, determination, and courage.

Old people don't suffer more or less than young people. Suffering comes upon us at any age. The only difference is that old people have experienced more of it simply because we have been alive longer. We have learned the hard way that suffering has a way of breaking down our ego-self and changing our priorities dramatically.

Our suffering teaches us compassion for the suffering of others. It draws our attention away from the inessential and focuses on that which matters most in the present. We have also learned that because suffering is a universal experience, it unifies us with all humanity. If nothing else, we are one in our suffering.

Difficult Memories

*The leaves of memory seemed to make
a mournful rustling in the dark.*
        Henry Wadsworth Longfellow

Even as we live our present moments consciously, we pause to remember moments from our past.

Some of what we recall brings a smile to our face because they are memories of fun and pleasant times; some of what comes to mind makes us recoil at the thought that we actually had to live through what we did.

Remembrance of the good times and bad is important to us because it provides us with a picture of continuity in our life and points to the causes and effects that resulted in who we are today.

These are days of remembrance, and the times of gathering our life. We have lived and loved, laughed and cried, and have known agony and joy. There are faces in our mind and memories in our heart. We remember them all; some with pleasure, some with pain.

Sometimes our past intrudes upon our present. Without invitation, memories that we would just as soon forget come crowding in to disturb our peace. They refuse to be forgotten and demand our full attention.

Some of us have intrusive memories that are simply irritating; others of us have memories that torment us. In either case, old age is the time to confront these haunting memories. Such confrontation is best done with the help of a professional who is willing to journey back with us to those dark times of our life. Sometimes the work we need to do includes self-forgiveness, and sometimes forgiveness of others. Always it includes reconciliation of our past with our present.

Visiting the past is not the same thing as living in the past. If we are perpetually thinking of days gone by we cheat ourselves out of the precious moments before us. If we are living in the past we are not living in the now. How tragic for us to be given life and not show up to receive it.

Memories are like safe-keeping depositories that hold bits and pieces of our journey through life. Once in a while it's important to open up those depositories and review our life a little. We do this without judging ourselves or getting bogged down in regrets. Rather, we "recollect" our life with a tolerant mind and a forgiving heart.

To recollect means more than to remember; it also means to collect again, to gather up, to recover or compose. In other words, we gather up and bring to mind all that we have been through, and we consider how it has affected us through the decades. We are, after all, the whole of our life experience, the sum of its parts. In light of the past, but grounded in the present, we compose ourselves anew.

Part Four
Contentment

*Everything has its wonders, even darkness
and silence, and I learn, whatever state I
may be in, therein to be content.*
Helen Keller

Wants

There are two ways to get enough. One is to continue to accumulate more and more. The other is to desire less.

G.K. Chesterton

Wanting is not the reason for our discontent; rather, it is to want more than we need and to crave that which can never satisfy us.

The problem with our wants comes when we begin to confuse them with who we are as human beings. We are beings in God, and when we remember that, we become conscious of our wants and of what prompts them. Yoked with God, the intensity of our wants diminishes and they become more manageable.

Old age has taught us to let go of our attachment to material possessions lest they end up owning us. Possession is not a problem for us, obsession is. Because we have learned to detach ourselves from the things we have enjoyed and which have brought us pleasure through the years, we are not devastated when they are taken away from us as we grow old. But our detachment can succeed only if, at the same time, we attach ourselves to something greater than what we release. This attachment is God.

Our goal is not to stop wanting. After all, wanting is our motivation for living and loving. Because we want to stay alive we take care of ourselves and stay away from danger. Because we want the welfare of our loved ones we act accordingly toward them. Our wants range from basic physical urges to evolved spiritual supplications.

Wants fuel our will and our will drives our life. Though we cannot ignore the power of wanting, our will, yoked with the will of God, steers us in paths of goodness and mercy. We subjugate all our wants to our heart's greatest desire – congruity with the will of God.

Knowing that nothing lasts forever emboldens us to let go of our attachments; and this in turn brings us contentment. But it seems paradoxical to believe in the impermanence of all form and, at the same time, to believe in the grace of contentment. How can we experience contentment when everything, including ourselves, is transitory? How can we be content when the very things we count on for our security may disappear tomorrow; and the conditions that meet our basic needs may change within the hour? For contentment to be experienced doesn't there have to be some form of permanence? Doesn't there have to be some assurance of longevity?

The reason that impermanence and contentment are not mutually exclusive is that impermanence is a physical condition, an external reality; while contentment is a spiritual condition, an internal reality.

Our contentment is not contingent on earthly circumstances. Our contentment does not depend on anything or anyone. Rather, it is rooted in our belief that we are one with God. Nothing can change that, not poverty, not illness, not even death.

Graced with contentment, we consider what we have to be sufficient. We honor and cherish the life before us no matter how simple or ordinary it may seem. Contentment leaves no room for coveting what we don't have or for envying those who have it. In contentment we want less and we make the best of what we already have. We take just enough, but no more.

Gratitude

If the only prayer you said was
thank you, that would be enough.
　　　　　　Meister Eckhart

By the time we reached old age we had already chased dreams and realized them; striven toward advancements and achieved them; and entertained desires and satisfied them.

Some would call this fulfillment, yet, there was still something missing for us. Dreams realized, advancements achieved, desires satisfied, what else did we want? Whatever it was, it was still "wanting." It was not until we transformed our mind and allowed our desire to give way to gratitude that we began to experience contentment. It was not until we stopped chasing, striving, and desiring and began thanking God for our bounty that we learned the secret of contentment.

On the path to contentment we surrender. That is, we drop our expectations of what should be and gratefully accept the hand that life has dealt us. On the path to contentment we open. We release our constricted heart, loosen our uptight mind, and ready ourselves for what is. On the path to contentment we receive. We no longer resist the inevitable, but instead gratefully receive our lot in life. On the path to contentment we detach. We drop our personal agendas and disengage from our ulterior motives. Instead we gratefully allow what comes to us and make the best of it.

We don't find contentment by looking to see what is missing from our life and attempting to obtain it. We look not to what is missing, but to what is present. Contentment is not about getting what we want, but wanting what we get. It is about realizing that once our basic needs are met, we want for nothing.

We may have urges, cravings, wishes, and desires, but these are not on the same level as needs. We can be appreciative when our basic needs are met, but satisfying our wants and desires only leads to more wants and more desires. Our needs can be satisfied, our wants and desires cannot.

Gratitude does not mean that we adopt passivity as a way of life, or that we acquiesce even to what we know to be wrong. Rather, gratitude means that, instead of struggling against the vicissitudes of life, we thankfully accept all that life presents to us with a humble heart and a realistic mind. We may still shed some tears initially or grumble a bit when bad things happen to us, but then we thank life for the good things, and we accept the good and the bad as part of life.

Contentment and discontentment are rooted in the attitude we adopt toward life. A contented person has a grateful heart; a malcontent is perpetually dissatisfied. Contentment comes not from espousing esoteric beliefs or ignoring the complexities of life, but from the simplicity of not knowing, yet believing; of not having, yet subsisting; and of not expecting, yet receiving.

With a grateful heart, we simplify our life; we make do with less; and we settle for what we need. With an appreciative heart, we stop comparing ourselves with others; and we drop away images of our ideal life. With an obliged heart, we accept others for who they are and for what they bring to the life we share. With a contented heart, we exude gratitude for all that is, for who we are, and for the world in which we live.

Acceptance

*The moment that judgment stops through
acceptance of what is, you are free of the mind. You
have made room for love, for joy, for peace.*
Eckhart Tolle

Old age is unpredictable.

When we least expect it, we may be hit
with a major crisis that impacts us greatly. It
may have to do with our health, our livelihood,
our personal security, a broken relationship, or
the death of a loved one. The crisis is usually
sudden and unexpected and catches us off
guard and unprepared.

We may attempt to respond to the crisis
by minimizing it, ignoring or denying it, or by
trying to escape it through abusive and
addictive behavior. But accepting a crisis
courageously means that we allow the natural
emotions that arise to be experienced and
expressed in a healthy manner. It means that
we accept the changes in our life that result
from the crisis, and we accept that, personally,
we will never be the same again.

To lament a plan gone awry or to feel disappointment when something on which we counted does not materialize is natural and understandable, yet to remain for long in the grip of discontent dulls our senses and diminishes our vitality. It is better to accept the actuality of what is and work from there. But before we accept the adverse circumstances in which we sometimes find ourselves, we must first ascertain their inevitability.

Gratuitous acceptance is not appropriate when intolerable circumstances are changeable. And acceptance does not mean wholesale condonation or acquiescence to the unhealthy conditions before us; it just means that we acknowledge the reality of what is.

We accept the times in our life when we have failed, that is, fallen short of what we expected of ourselves. We accept our failures as opportunities to learn from our mistakes. We accept that some of our dreams have gone unrealized. We are disappointed, but then we go on to dream new dreams and work toward their realization.

We are guided by the wisdom of our soul. We may be asked to accept what is and to make the most of it, or we may be encouraged to push for change. Courage is not the denial of circumstances; rather, it is the force within us that empowers us to overcome them. But sometimes it takes more courage to accept what is, without attempting to change it, than to fight for change.

Acceptance of life as it presents itself to us is not the same as resignation or submissive acquiescence. Acceptance is facing the reality of what is, and finding a way to make it work. In our old age we learn that surrendering to the inevitable, while sometimes hard to do, brings us release, relief, and contentment. We feel the release of the intensive energy we have been exerting to get our way. We experience relief because letting go of our inordinate desire for a particular outcome frees us to accept whatever comes. And we are graced with contentment because it is the fruit of acceptance.

Contentment

Contentment is the only real wealth.
Albert Nobel

Contentment is that ineffable capacity of the soul to be with what is.

In the mindset of contentment we are no longer anxious about what might happen to us. Instead, we calmly accept what is now. The peace of contentment gives us clarity of mind to live our moments fully, without the distraction of envy, yearning, or inordinate desire.

Joy, bliss, ecstasy, rapture, pleasure, and elations are feelings of great delight and supreme happiness, but they are not the same as contentment. The difference is that the experience of these emotions is contingent upon external forces, while the experience of contentment comes from an internal state of being. Even satisfaction differs from contentment. Satisfaction depends on the fulfillment of a desire, while contentment can be experienced even without a desire being met.

As we grow old we are not content to live our life for our sake alone. It is not enough for us to desire and obtain that which does not last. Our decades of life have taught us that there is more to life than power, pleasure, and prestige. We have also been exposed to vulnerability, pain, and humiliation. What is more important to us now is the faith to persevere through the storms of life, the courage to confront the obstacles that arise in old age, and the humility to accept what comes.

There is a way that we can live our old age with equanimity in the midst of chaos, presence in the midst of distraction, and authenticity in the midst of superficiality. It is the way of contentment.

Try as we may, we cannot conjure up the state of contentment at will. We cannot acquire it from external sources or pray it into being. We can't even earn it through our good behavior, and we don't deserve it because of our faithfulness. We are graced with contentment simply because it is the true nature of our soul.

Contentment does not mean that we "clench our teeth and bear" whatever happens in our life. Rather, it means that when things are going badly for us we are prepared to cope, always returning to God in prayer and meditation for the strength and courage to make the best of it. There is no sweeter contentment than to be yoked with the essence of God. Ultimately, contentment is prompted by our belief that God is the essence of our existence and the purpose of our life.

Enough

*Those who know that enough is
enough will always have enough.*
Lao Tzu

It would have been enough.

For more than a thousand years the
Jewish people have sung the Dayenu, a song of
gratitude, appreciation, and contentment. One
stanza of the song proclaims: *It would have been
enough for us...* In other words, it would have
been sufficient, and yet, we received even
more.

In our old age we recognize and
acknowledge the extent of our own blessings,
and we add them to the words, *It would have
been enough...*

It would have been enough to be
granted life in this world; but we also received
a purpose that made our life worth living.

It would have been enough to be given a
mind with which to function; but we also
received a heart with which to feel compassion
for those who suffer.

It would have been enough to have bestowed on us a body to move and act and have our being; but we also received a spirit with which to animate our soul.

It would have been enough to know the love of our family and friends; but we also received the love of God.

Part Five
Abundant Life

Each part of life has its own abundant harvest, to be garnered in season. Old age is rich in blessings.
                                    Cicero

Purpose

The purpose of human life is to serve, and to show compassion and the will to help others.
Albert Schweitzer

Each life, however long it may last, is unique and has a purpose to fulfill.

Whether it is a newborn that lives only for moments or a person of many decades, heaven ordains a purpose for that life. Whether we are like the hibiscus flower that blooms magnificently for one day and then perishes or the perennial redwood tree that stands majestically for eons, our life is of great consequence regardless of its endurance.

We have little control over the length of our life, but we have much control over how we respond to the opportunities our life offers to us. Actually, just being, even if only for a moment, fulfills the purpose of our life. A single moment of a life contains in it the whole of its potential and the fullness of its possibility. Life is life whether fleeting or protracted, and heaven and earth rejoice at every conception and mourn at every death.

A life without involvement is not a life; but a life that gives of itself, even unto death, for the sake of love, bears the fruit of God. Even if our life is structured by responsibilities and prescribed by circumstances, we can reach beyond the shallow and mundane to find a way to give purpose to our existence. As long as we are responding to the graciousness of our soul and the promptings of our spirit, we are attending to the purpose of our life.

Our soul withers when it is left to meander through lost moments in search of nothing; in love with no one; involved with meaningless trivialities. Attending to the purpose of our life we know what matters most to us and what matters least, and we live our life accordingly.

The purpose of our life does not end or fade away just because we become old and feeble, or even demented. Even when our mind can no longer be attentive, our soul continues to attend.

Attention

Attention taken to its highest degree, is the same
thing as prayer, it presupposes faith and love.
Simone Weil

The greatest responsibility that comes with life
is that we attend to it. This is especially true
when the number of our days is measured.

When we live attentively we live with
intention and appreciation. Life is fragile and
ephemeral; it is granted to us in small portions
to be lived purposefully. Living with attention
we do one thing at a time; and we attend to
what is before us. At the end of the day, that to
which we have given our attention becomes
our life experience.

At the crux of our life there is a conflict
between conscious, attentive living and
unconscious, cursory living. There is a marked
difference between stringing a series of events
together and calling it life, and actually
experiencing life and all that it brings.

Thoughts, emotions, and the busyness
of living can fill the unattended life, but not

fulfill it. When our mind is focused on yesterday or tomorrow we are virtually unconscious. Only by attending to what is before us now can we live consciously.

There is no question that in our youth we squandered some of our precious time on earth. We have probably lived unconsciously most of our life. But now, in our old age, we are conscious most of the time; and we live each day with full attention.

Attending to our life, we dare to stay in ordinary moments. It is then that we discover God, who is willing to just be there with us with no spectacular show for us to witness and no sign with which to impress us. Hallowed be the ordinary, regular, usual, plain, undistinguished, customary, and normal moments, for such is the essence of our life.

Attending to our life has less to do with finding ourselves and more with losing ourselves in something beyond us. It has to do less with discovering the boundaries of our identity and more with transcending those boundaries and moving toward a fuller measure of our being.

When we attend to our life we follow the ultimate desire of our heart, and our action reflects the strongest conviction of our mind. We actuate love-energy into deeds.

Simplicity

If one's life is simple, contentment has to come.
Dalai Lama

Simplicity is authentic, transparent, humble, refreshing, and beautiful.

There is nothing as powerful as simplicity. Our life becomes simpler when we stop trying to conform it to what we want; when we let it play out as it will; and when we respond to it wholeheartedly.

We simplify our life in every way we can, always remembering that less is more, and that simplicity begins in the heart. Life is simple when we work through burdensome memories, leave behind worrisome predictions, and focus on the moment before us. The more we let go, the simpler our life becomes. Life may be unpredictable, but the spirit within us is not.

Simplicity does not mean that we deny our basic human needs. Self-love compels us to take care of ourselves by providing the minimal necessities, such as food and drink, shelter and hygiene, and protection from physical or psychic pain.

Simplicity means that we know when enough is enough. But we have to be careful because though we may have all that we need, one instance of lamentation over what we don't have will throw us into discontent.

How ironic it is that the less we have, the more grateful we are for what we have; but the more we have, the more we want. Our covetousness for what we don't have drowns out our gratitude for what we do.

In our later life we awaken to the fulfillment of emptiness. What a paradox it is that to receive the fullness of life we must first give away all that we desperately cling to. What an irony that we spend our days searching the world over for that which will take away our pain and make us happy, while the treasure we seek is not outside us but within us.

We yearned for that which would satisfy our senses and provide what was missing from our life. We accumulated possessions, power, and prestige; and we collected experiences, ideas, and religions in hope of some contentment. But all our effort was in vain. It was not until we surrendered our illusions of self-sufficiency and separate existence, and realized our oneness with all that is that we could be content.

We turn within and delve into the depths of our being where we can be who we truly are – the reflection of God. We enter here empty-handed; accepting of what is, forgiving of everything, trusting in God, grateful for life, and prepared to die.

Equanimity

We age inevitably; the old joys fade away and are gone; and at last comes equanimity and the flame burning clear.
James Oppenheim

Equanimity is rooted in the acceptance of what is.

It is our attitude toward life that accepts whatever experiences come and makes the best of them while, at the same time, keeping our composure.

Equanimity is the clarity of mind with which we are graced to look upon every being without prejudice or judgment. It is our decision to love all beings and to treat them with kindness and generosity at every opportunity.

In our younger years we spent much of our time and energy grasping for what we wanted and pushing away what we detested. The equanimity that we acquire in old age allows us to just experience what is, without rejecting it or attaching ourselves to it. We develop equanimity by staying grounded in our essential self even through the many ups and downs, twists and turns, which we encounter in our old age.

When we allow equanimity into our life, we remain fully engaged. Rather than adopt an attitude of indifference or one of bias, we remain composed and balanced, embracing all life equally. Allowing equanimity to take front and center in our life does not do away with the problems that arise with old age, but it gives us the composure to deal with them consciously and responsibly.

The equanimity that we acquire in old age is like climbing to the top of a mountain to get a better, more panoramic view of what is. Rather than the myopic perspective to which we are limited when standing in the mire of our own desires and biases, equanimity provides us with a more fair and balanced picture to consider. The bigger picture results in better discernment for us.

Part Six
The Ways of Love

To love is to attach oneself to the spirit of unity.
Abraham Heschel

Wisdom

By three methods we may learn wisdom: first by reflection, which is noblest; second by imitation, which is easiest; and third by experience, which is the bitterest.

Confucius

Old people do not have a monopoly on wisdom, far from it.

There is, however, something to be said for the many decades of life we have experienced, including the many mistakes we have made and the failures we have sustained. This has given us a broad perspective on life and living that certainly contributes to wisdom. But of course, no matter how many years of experience we accumulate, wisdom does not come to us unless we are wholeheartedly involved in life and constantly attentive to what life teaches us.

Wisdom reveals to us the ways of life. It comes to offer us awareness beyond the grasp of our senses and the power of our reason. It teaches us to gain from suffering, to grow from difficulty, and to raise forgiveness from the ashes of anger and hate. It teaches us to accept what is, and to dream of what can be. It reveals to us the potency of the moment before us; and composes us with contentment as we face the agony and ecstasy of our daily life.

We ascended the mountain looking for enlightenment, and searched the caves of comprehension. We tore at the veil of mystery, and descended into the depths of meaning. But wisdom eluded us and our effort was in vain. Yet, in the midst of silent prayer and the openness of faith, wisdom rises from vacuity to light our path of life.

Wisdom brings peace to the warring factions of our being; and heals our wound of separation. It unites within us the external with the internal; joins the new with the old; and reconciles the darkness with the light. Wisdom infuses love into our heart and gives birth to an understanding that we've never known before.

Forgiveness

*That's one thing we learn as
we grow old – how to forgive.*
L.M. Montgomery

Looking back from our old age we realize that we have made mistakes.

We have accumulated regrets and built up guilt; and we realize that to regret past actions or lost opportunities is the first part of repentance. The second part is to learn from our mistakes and to correct our course. But to stay stuck in the mire of guilt over what we have done or failed to do serves no one, least of all God.

We have learned that it is better to acknowledge the reality of our errancy, experience our profound remorse, and accept forgiveness from God, ourselves, and from those whom we have harmed. When we let go of the burdens that bog down our soul and inhibit our spirit, we release all that keeps open the wounds of our heart. As we forgive ourselves and others, and let go of past hurts;

new life enters in, along with new risks and new possibilities for living and loving more abundantly.

Our decision to forgive is made cognitively, but the forgiveness is made spiritually. Behold the forgiving heart; it reflects the heart of God. Our forgiving heart promotes the healing of memories that haunt us even into old age.

As we head toward the edge of life we begin to jettison the burdensome debts we hold against ourselves and others. Otherwise, the bitter energy within us poisons our soul and makes it very difficult for us to make peace with ourselves, the world, and God before we die.

Forgiveness is transforming.

Envisioning our death, whether from near or far, prompts us to begin the transformation. One by one, we remember the nature of injuries perpetrated against us. One by one, we decide to no longer hold them against our wrongdoers. It makes no difference if they don't deserve our forgiveness, and that they have not earned it. It makes no difference if they have not repented, much less asked for our forgiveness. All that matters is that we decide to forgive them. We still hold them accountable for their actions; and they still have to suffer the consequences of their behavior, but that is not inconsistent with forgiveness. We do not forgive them because it is something we should do; we forgive them because we are ready to take back our life.

Love

Those who love deeply never grow old;
they may die of old age, but they die young.
Sir Arthur Wing Pinero

A life hoarded for its own sake is already dead;
but a life given away in the name of love is
everlasting.

In our old age we encounter new
limitations every day, yet nothing stops us
from responding to our divine calling: to love
one another.

We are sent into the world in the name
of God to love those who have not known love,
to accept those who have been rejected, to heal
those who have been wounded, and to be with
those who have been abandoned.

It is true, the older we get the more
fragile our life becomes, and the more we have
to tend to ourselves just to stay alive. But our
life cannot be just about us.

Our love for God compels us to
withdraw from earthly attachments and to
invest our time, energy, and attention in the

well-being of others. The more we love God, the more we love our fellow-beings. Love overtakes us like a powerful tsunami, leveling our ego defenses, dissolving our selfish tendencies, and liberating us to do the work of God.

No matter how much schooling we may have had or how much knowledge we possess, old age is the real school of higher learning. Perhaps it's because the lessons make more sense to us now. Perhaps it's because we are paying more attention; or maybe it's because our mind is more open to learning.

In our old age we want to be understood, but even more, we want to understand. Before we die we want to know, not the secret of the universe, but the secret of the heart. We want to discover, not the esoteric concept of infinity, but the definite power of love. We want to believe, not in the promise of eternity, but in the certainty of the present moment. In our old age we are prepared to learn and to apply the lessons of love in our own life and in the lives of those whom we serve.

From the vantage point of old age, we love life and all who live it. It becomes more and more clear to us that we are one with all beings. We see the universal aspect of existence, yet, we are also aware of the uniqueness of each individual being. Our vision of the whole does not preclude our vision of the parts.

By the time we reached old age we had already learned that no one is indispensable. But we have also learned that everyone is irreplaceable. Not one of us, regardless of whether we are useful and productive or not, can be replaced when we are gone. This is because we are each original and unique. In the history of the universe no one has ever lived who was exactly like us. And into infinity, no one ever will be.

In our old age we no longer place our faith on words alone. We have learned over the years that love is more than sentimental declarations; it is action. We cannot love without giving away something that is ours: our time, our energy, our attention, our intimacy, our possessions, our will, our life.

Self-love

You yourself, as much as anybody in the entire universe, deserve your love and affection.
Buddha

Taking care of ourselves is smart, but it is also a sign of self-love.

Growing old is the period of our life in which we can finally stop to rest and reflect, pray and meditate, enjoy silence and solitude, waste time and take stock.

We have learned that our body needs to be loved by us; the rest follows from that. For some of us, however, it took growing old to truly appreciate how miraculous our body is.

As we began to notice the wear and tear that our physical being had sustained through the decades, we realized that our body was not a renewable resource. In our youth, some of us thought it was and we took advantage of it. We worked hard and we played hard, and we didn't always take good care of ourselves.

In our later years we have had to be more careful lest we lose even what we have left. Of course, the aging process cannot be denied; and we will eventually lose our physical abilities. But in the meantime, we protect our body like the treasure it is.

If we did not know it before, old age has taught us through sometimes harsh lessons, that eating healthy food and getting plenty of exercise is crucial maintenance. Adequate rest is just as important.

How do we love ourselves in our old age? What is it that we do to live life to the best of our ability? We determine which of our daily practices affect us detrimentally and we put a stop to them. This requires discipline, to be sure, and a deep respect for the law of cause and effect. Everything we do or desist from doing has a positive or negative consequence.

Unhealthy behaviors and addictions follow us into old age. These include any behaviors that we know to be detrimental to our well-being, but are unable to control. Some of these are the abusive consumption of alcohol or other drugs (prescription or nonprescription), smoking, and eating disorders.

While growing old is not a cause of addiction, the loneliness, isolation, and depression that we sometimes experience in old age, can contribute to the problem. We love ourselves by asking for help with our addictions from family, friends, and groups that are dedicated to help. Of course, the greatest help comes from within.

We love ourselves when we use the time we have been given effectively. This includes doing plenty of stress-reducing activities like playing, resting, and meditating. And we decide not to hold against ourselves or others our past actions or inactions. In other words, we forgive.

Just as we respond to the needs of others, we respond to our own needs. We have always had needs and those needs continue into old age. We grow old and our energy declines, but our need for purpose, personal involvement, and participation in community never wanes. We also need to experience and express the emotions we feel as a result of growing old, including grief, fear, doubt, and loneliness.

We love ourselves by remembering that we are precious in the eyes of God and then treating ourselves accordingly.

Part Seven
Essential Being

In time, essence becomes a permanent and abiding presence, and the person progressively identifies with it as his true nature and identity. It becomes the ordinary experience of the individual every minute of his life. The fullness of essence is then permanently present and is the center and the source of the individual's life and actions.

A.H. Almaas

Spirituality

If wrinkles must be written upon your brows, let them not be written upon your heart. The spirit should not grow old.
                                    James Garfield

We do not use spirituality to escape from the vicissitudes that come with old age.

On the contrary, spirituality, which is connecting with our soul, compels us to confront life directly and immediately as it unfolds before us. Living spiritually opens our eyes to the reality of what is, and opens our heart to deal with it with loving kindness, compassion, and equanimity.

If the first part of our life was about our body, that is, surviving and thriving; and the middle part of our life was about our mind, that is, developing our intellect and learning; then perhaps the last part of our life is about our spirit, that is, opening to the essence of our existence and realizing the purpose of our life.

Because the experience of growing old shakes us to our foundation and demands of us that we be authentic, it is not unusual for us to begin considering our unexamined beliefs at this stage of our life. If, for example, we adopted a particular set of beliefs that was either passed on to us as children or to which we pledged our life early in our adulthood, but which we never seriously questioned; we may begin to question it now.

This is by no means a spiritual crisis, but merely an opportunity in our old age to examine our spirituality in the light of who we are now and what we believe in our heart of hearts.

Turning to our spiritual life as we grow old is not just a matter of reading holy books or attending religious services. It is not limited to blissful feelings or theological understandings. Rather, the spiritual life to which we are drawn includes the marriage of our divine and human natures.

Our spiritual life includes celestial joy as well as earthly sorrow; faith and trust as well as doubt and fear. It is a sacred dimension in which our finiteness and infiniteness are unified, and our essential self and God are one.

In prayer and meditation we open our mind and heart to the essence of our being. We place our attention on the moment before us, and we breathe and listen. We listen to the silence. How ironic that rather than enter into meditation in order to learn the secrets of life or to discover the mysteries of the universe, we meditate to enter into the way of unknowing.

As we grow old we enter into a deeper spirituality. We are more disciplined in our pursuit of serenity. We spend more time in silent solitude, not verbalizing prayers as much as listening prayerfully.

Alone and still, we enter the center point of our existence. It is to this sacred place that we go to get away from the forces that distract us from our essential self. It is here that we turn our back on the demands and expectations that hound us. It is here that the stronghold of our deceitful self is broken and its pieces are dissolved into authenticity. It is here that our thoughts and feelings fall away and we experience the true nature of our soul.

Meditation

Meditation is the dissolution of thoughts in eternal awareness or pure consciousness without objectification, knowing without thinking, merging finitude in infinity.
Voltaire

Like the sunflower that turns naturally to the sun for sustenance, our soul seeks out the countenance of God.

As the light of the sun aliments the flower, the love of God nourishes our soul. The flower opens to receive the gift of life and our soul opens to receive the spirit of God.

We yearn for divine union and wholeness of being, and when we meditate our soul opens to the eternal presence and influence of God. In meditation the mind attends to the will of God, the heart opens to the love of God, and our body disposes itself to the service of God.

Our soul cannot build its nest among the noises of the world; it does not stay in the midst of busyness, compulsivity, or superficiality. It needs time to retreat, reflect, and replenish. It feels at home where the only expectation is to be.

When we slow our pace and stop to rest a while, and when we set down the burdens we carry, we are prepared to meditate. When we remember to breathe and forget to think, we can begin to meditate.

In meditation we stop what we are doing and take the time to recollect ourselves. We meditate by giving our total attention to one thing only – the spirit of God that manifests through our breath. When we are distracted by the sounds around us, and by the incessant thoughts that bombard our mind and detract our attention from the here and now, we simply acknowledge the sounds, identify them, and return to conscious breathing. We observe the thoughts dispassionately and detachedly and, no matter what enters our mind, we simply acknowledge it and return to conscious breathing.

In the profundity of our meditation we enter into communion with God. We descend to the depths of our being and experience the full dimension of our nature. In communion we uncover our divine roots, yet, we are more human than ever. Rather than leave the world to be with God, we are propelled into the thick of our humanity to behold the face of God in every soul. Even as we hear the voice of our

Beloved, we hear the cries of those who suffer in the world. Our communion with God prepares us to re-enter a world of strife and destitution to be of service to our fellow beings.

We find that we cannot go for long without returning to the fountain of our sustenance. As a lover longs for the ecstatic intimacy of the beloved, our soul longs for the presence of God. This holy communion is consummated in the constant, conscious connection between the finite and the infinite. In love we surrender ourselves totally and completely to a life in God.

Old Soul, Young Spirit

There are victories of the soul and spirit.
Sometimes even if you lose, you win.
Elie Wiesel

We have an old soul, yet it is eternally young in spirit.

In our youth we worked hard to construct a self-image that would impress even the angels. What's worse, we probably mistook that self-image for our true identity.

Fortunately, as we grew old we began to set aside that which was not real and to embrace that which was. In our old age we have stopped looking into the mirror to see who we are. Instead, we look into our innermost self and there we come to know our soul.

Our soul has known us and accepted us from before we were born. Before we accept the circumstances of our life, we must first accept the totality of who we are. We take back those parts of ourselves that we have disowned, including those we consider dark, animalistic, and primordial. We do not choose between the good and evil in us; we do not select the beautiful and leave behind the ugly.

We accept our creativeness along with our destructiveness; we face the lightness of our being as well as the darkness; nothing is hidden and nothing is judged.

Our soul is the essence of God within us; it is who we are at our deepest level. It is not a thing, but a dimension of being that colors our life. It is our most intimate and private self and, at the same time, it is what we have in common with all beings. At the level of our soul, we are connected with everyone who has ever lived, lives now, or will ever live.

Our soul is the fountain of love and God is the source from which it draws. Love is our soul's dynamic response to life. It is complete and profound, and when we are connected with our soul we also love this way. Love becomes for us the reason to exist and the purpose to live.

Our soul is the matrix of our spiritual life. It is not held to any limits, but moves out beyond the finite to the infinite. It bridges the actual with the ephemeral; transforms the moment into eternity; and synthesizes the physical and the spiritual. It takes the mundane and makes it sublime; and what is limited it makes transcendent.

Our soul immerses us in the rawness of life, yet it inspires us to transcend our humanity. It exposes us to the ordinary and the commonplace, yet reveals to us the sacred and the divine. Wisdom and grace, intuition and sensibility, love and imagination, these are the elements of our soul. Our soul reveres life, yet it grounds us in the certitude of our mortality.

Beauty

Love is the beauty of the soul.
St. Augustine

Old age is harsh sometimes and can wear an ugly mask.

We turn away with repulsion, hoping the grotesque will be gone when we look back. But it is still there and it is real. There are moments, precious moments, when the beauty of creation comes to save us from despair. Suddenly there's a flower protruding from the weeds, offering itself in all its glory. The early morning mist graces us with a mystical vision that we carry with us through the day.

Beauty is all around us ready to move our heart, inspire our mind, and refresh our soul. Sometimes, when we are paying close attention, beauty manifests where we least expect it.

Beauty is the nature of God infused into all dimensions of being. It is the likeness of God that gives beyond measure and touches us profoundly. Beauty is the heavenly stimulus that inspires us to be co-creators of living art. We know the nature of God not through knowledge or even wisdom, but through the beauty of all we survey. God animates our soul through beauty; and we, in turn, offer our inner beauty to the world.

In our search for beauty we learn that beauty is everywhere if only we recognize it. In our prayer we ask that the heavens be opened to reveal to us the glory of God; but all we see is a tiny hummingbird flying to and fro, reflecting the lighting of the sun.

We believe that God is beautiful and we want to be shown even a glimpse of that beauty; but all we see is the face of an old man smiling gently at us as he passes on the sidewalk.

We want to feast our eyes on spectacular visions; but all we see are the earthly angels tending to the sick and starving masses.

We want to behold the beauty of far away cities that have not been bombed into oblivion; but all we see are children playing innocently in the rubble of war, delighting in their childhood while they still can.

The beauty of God manifests in the remarkably gorgeous; but God's beauty is also in ordinary, commonplace, everyday manifestations of creation. We experience the beauty of God every day regardless of where we are or what may be before us. When we recognize the exquisiteness of God in the wrinkled face of an old woman, then we know true beauty.

Part Eight
Befriending Death

There is but one freedom, to put oneself right with death. After that everything is possible.
                                        Albert Camus

Awareness of Death

*The years seem to rush by now, and I think of death
as a fast approaching end of a journey – double and
treble the reason for loving as well as working while
it is day.*

George Eliot

Awareness of our mortality radically enlivens us and prompts us to live each moment of our life deliberately.

As we have grown old we have developed a sense of temporality. When we were young we took longevity for granted. We assumed that we had time without end to do whatever we wanted. We were not conscious of the impermanence of life. We planned for times that never came; we waited for occasions that never happened; and we strove for goals that vanished like mirages once we reached them. We worked hard to make a living; we founded organizations; wrote books; and built a reputation; but in the light of death, now none of that seems to matter as much as loving and being loved.

Now the decisions we make and the actions we take are influenced by a new reality – our time is running out. It may not be tomorrow that the end will come, but we know it is not far off. We feel a sense of urgency, but without panic or haste. Rather, we have awareness that we are living our last chapter.

Toward the end of our life death begins to flirt with us, exposing us to quick glimpses of its expansive peace; and reminding us that, in the light of death, all else loses its urgency and importance. Death breaks into our life occasionally to teach us how to die before we die.

At the core of our existence is our soul, which is neither born nor dies. When we are conscious of our soul we do not fear death because our essence is immune from the reaping. Anchored in the essence of our existence, we can walk through the storms of life and suffer at the hands of evil, yet never lose our integrity, our original innocence, or our wholeness. Only God, who gave rise to our soul in life, can absorb it again in death.

It seems that in the homestretch of our life our focal point is love; love of our family and friends, love of life, and love of God. Nothing matters now except the connections of our heart. Just the thought of never again looking upon those whom we love, never again listening to their voices or embracing them, is enough to cast us into the deep abyss of sorrow and grief. And yet, this is the reality of death.

Our awareness of death keeps us attentive to how we treat others whom we love. Every word we speak, every gesture we make, and every interaction we have with those who share our life we frame in love. Even during the difficult times with interpersonal relations, we remember that everything pales in the light of eternity except the love we give to one another.

As we prepare to die we are devastated by radical loss. On our passage toward death we weep not for ourselves, but for those whom we must leave behind. We have been rooted in the soil of love, and now death uproots us and blows us away like grass on the fields.

Awareness of our inexorable death sentence compels us to live authentically. We don't have time to waste on fantasy or pretext. Our awareness of death evokes honesty and unpretentiousness. In fact, the closer death comes to us, the more genuine and humble we become.

Remembering our forthcoming death also helps us to set our priorities in life. In the light of death, that which is truly significant rises to the top of our list, while the less significant drops to the bottom. Living in congruence with our values and investing our time, energy, and resources in accordance with what is most important to us brings wholeness, even in the face of death.

At the end of our life, regardless of the circumstances that our loved ones face, all we can do before we go is commend them to God and to one another. How blessed our life, how sacred our time together. Yet, from these temporal gifts comes that which will not be taken from us – the permanence of love. No matter how hard we work or how much we accomplish in life, at the hour of our death, what matters most is the love we hold in our heart.

Fear of Death

The fear of death follows from the fear of life. A person who lives fully is prepared to die at any time.
Mark Twain

Old age prompts us to contemplate the reality of death.

Intellectually, we are aware that it is imminent, but emotionally we keep it at bay because we are afraid. Our fear of death prompts us to seek illusory moorings to secure our life. We may amass power, property, and prestige in an attempt to rise above the inevitability of death. We may busy ourselves in mind and body lest we appear already dead. We dare not stop to catch our breath or move too slowly for our own good; we fear the hound of death will overcome us unless we live with haste. We plan ahead believing that time is on our side; our faith is in tomorrow, for we dare not face today.

We hope that if we're good and decent death will look away; or if we pray the whole night through we will be spared the scythe. But death does not negotiate with us. It comes when it comes, ready or not, sometimes with no rhyme or reason.

What is it that we fear about death? For some of us it is the idea of complete annihilation, of no longer existing. For others, it is about entering into a mystery, an unknown state of being. For others of us, it is not death that we fear, but the prelude to death through which we must pass. We fear the pain, the helplessness, and the aloneness we will feel in those final moments.

Although our fear of death is normal and even necessary to help us stay alive, inordinate fear of death can inhibit living fully. That kind of fear keeps us from responding spontaneously to life. Instead, we are left reacting compulsively to it. Befriending death, on the other hand, allays our fear and allows us to transform our life.

Even if death is not near, we know that old age is the prelude to that dark night. Growing old seems to expand our horizons and free our inhibitions, but it also introduces a sense of pressure into our life. We have always known that we are susceptible to dying at any age, but now we know that the possibility has come nearer. Now every moment counts.

Even if we are not afraid of death, our love of life manifests as resistance to anything that threatens its continuation, whether it be disease, old age, or external assault. Perhaps it is because life is transient and short-lived that it is so precious to us, especially in our old age when there is so little of it left to live. Perhaps it is precious because it is the incarnation of God in the world. Perhaps life is precious to us because it is an opportunity to love and be loved.

It isn't that old people have a death wish. On the contrary, we want to live. Life is too valuable to give it up so easily; but we do think about death and about how much closer to us it is today than it was yesterday. But the imminence of death is not what frightens us the most; rather, our fear is that death might come before we have truly lived.

We will accept death whenever it comes because we have befriended it in our daily life. We will welcome death as a blessing because we believe that it leads to a total union with God. We will release our hold on being because we know that God will always be. Opening ourselves to death; surrendering ourselves individually; and relinquishing our entitlement to existence; transforms our fear of death into a great anticipation of eternal oneness in God.

Dying

*...life and death are one, even as
the river and the sea are one...*
Kahlil Gibran

In old age we begin preparing for death.

We start to let go of all the burdens that
bog down our soul and inhibit our spirit. We
start to release our hold on those things which
we will not take with us: our property, our
power, and our prestige.

We abandon once and for all any hatred,
resentment, anger, or guilt which we may be
harboring. We relinquish anything that keeps
open the wounds of our heart.

As we contemplate our death, we leave
behind all that we have accumulated through
the years, not just the things we have
possessed, but also our pride, prejudice, and
the stories we've told ourselves. We forsake
our work, our plans, our dreams, and our
expectations of what should be. And, although
we must leave behind the physical presence of

all whom we have loved, we do not leave behind the love, for it is of our essence and it will never die.

We have been as a flower in the garden of God. Born of earth and water, air and fire; we bloomed where we were planted; and we blossomed into who we were meant to be. We brought beauty into the world, if only for a season. The world was graced with our existence, and blessed with our presence. And now our petals fade and our leaves begin to wither. The flower sears and then it dies. Its seed falls to the earth and blooms again in God.

The meaning of our life has manifested in the way we have lived, in the choices we have made, and in the priorities we have set and followed. Now the time of our dying has meaning too. It means that we have come to the end of our personal journey. It means that we have finished our work in this world. It means that we can relinquish all that attaches us to human life, and open ourselves to receive eternal life.

Dying means that we no longer need our body or our mind; only our soul; which never dies. Our dying is not a physical failure, but a spiritual success. It is ordained that all that is born must also die. Our body, then, is merely following the law of nature. It is ordained that all which is of the spirit is everlasting. Our soul and the love it holds will never die.

Our time of dying is the most intimate experience of our life. Because these moments could be our last, they are precious and deserving of our full attention. Intimate moments allow us to be ourselves without fear of being judged. They invite openness and honesty. They are liberating because now we have nothing left to lose.

In the light of our impending death, we are conscious of the intricacies of life, including the ordinary things around us. Faced with death, we become more alive than ever. We accept the gifts life hands to us and we enjoy them fully before we have to let them go. As we enter the penultimate days of our life, many emotions rush our mind. We allow them to come and we allow them to go.

We are one with our dying as we have been one with our living. We enter our dying time without trepidation or regret. As we release all that binds us to life, we experience our indescribable harmony with the universe and with all that is. We are no longer separated from anything, but in union with all creation. We discard our guilt; we make peace with the world; and we love with all our heart.

Our heart breaks as we anticipate our death. There is so much to live for, yet so little time left; so much love to be given, and so much love to receive. Even before we die we have already lost so much. Our body is limited in movement, our mind is sometimes cloudy, and our world has become so small. So much is lost, yet the core of our being is never lost. We cling to that which cannot perish.

Because we are unique, our way of living and our way of dying is also unique. Only we know exactly what we are thinking and feeling as we face imminent death. Nothing said or written can presume to know our personal experience in living or dying.

We do not fear the shadow of death that overtakes us even as we celebrate our life, for it portends for us a life in God. We do not fear cessation of our being, for it is through the death of our humanity that our soul claims its divinity. We do not fear what awaits us on the other side of midnight, for whatever its nature may be; it is the home from whence we came. It is the union of our soul with the essence of God. It is the part returning to the whole, where all is one and one is all.

As we enter into the deepest darkness, we will begin to see with the greatest clarity. Rationality will not help our understanding, and our senses will no longer aid our perception of what is real. Instead, we will know the divine mystery because we will be a part of it.

We wait for what must be. We wait for the transformation of our life. Our separate, single self will begin to lose its boundaries and a sense of unity and oneness will overcome us. Gradually, what we have known to be will begin to disappear. We will be free of the tethers of worldly existence. We will no longer be bound by the restraints of time or space, state or dimension. We open to the nothingness that comes; we embrace the darkness that comes before the light.

It is all right for us to let go of what has been. We don't need it anymore. We surrender into heavenly peace. We allow the love of God to envelop us. We go gently into the holy night. We release all that we have been and enter bare and poor into the ineffable darkness. We welcome the dying of the light for it proclaims the reality of infinite being. We are absorbed into the sacred silence of eternity. We enter into the sanctifying stillness where we will know the essence of all that is. We let go of our blessed soul, for now it abides in God.

Legacy

What you leave behind is not what is engraved in stone monuments, but what is woven into the lives of others.

Pericles

Even in our finiteness, we transcend ourselves and we transcend our life by what we leave behind when we die.

We give of ourselves through the life we lead, the ideas we pass on, the treatment we afford others, and the presence of God that we share with the world.

Few persons are remembered for long after they die. But, while the memory of who we were may blow away like dry leaves in winter, the contributions we make today, whether for good or bad, will impact the world for ages to come.

Whether we realize it or not, we affect persons whom we will never meet by how we live our life today. Attending purposefully to our life is crucial because the decisions we make now, individually and collectively, about our life, about our family, about our environment, about world hunger, about war and disease, will touch the lives of persons living centuries into the future. They won't know who we were, but they will be blessed or cursed by what we did or failed to do.

Even as we accept our impermanence, we wonder what will come after us; what kind of world will exist after we are gone. Our world has changed so much since our parents died. What changes will come in the aftermath of our death? In any case, whatever changes come, they will not affect us. It seems strange to consider that the world will go on, but we will not be here to witness it.

As we approach the end of our life, we acquire a deep respect and appreciation for the mountains and the valleys, the rivers and the trees, the sun and the moon, and the planets and the stars. Although we can only imagine how long ago these manifestations of divine creativity were formed and how long they will exist, one thing we know for sure: they will be here far beyond the end of our own individual life.

This realization is both comforting and sad for us. It is comforting because God's handiwork will continue to be here for billions of souls to behold; yet sad because we will no longer be here to delight in it.

We were fortunate in our youth that those of older generations were generative with us. Parents, grandparents, aunts and uncles, teachers, coaches, bosses, and others taught us; mentored us; and guided us as we struggled to negotiate life. Now, in our old age, it is our turn to pass on to others the benefit of what we have learned through the decades of our life.

We have the privilege, honor, and responsibility to nurture and guide those of younger generations. We may offer our generativity to our children, grandchildren, or others who look to us for direction and inspiration. We offer them wisdom, experience, and concern for their well-being. We are like a mountain lake that receives the melting snow from on high and streams it to the valley below, fostering life along the way.

In our old age we realize that we are getting ready to become ancestors to our children and their children's children and grandchildren. We start thinking about our ancestors. Before they became ancestors they were old like us.

What an astonishing realization it is for us that we are the link between the past and the future. Life is like a relay race. We took the baton from our ancestors who had taken it from their ancestors, and we pass it on to our posterity. They, in turn, will pass it on to those who follow them. How amazing it is that, although we will never know our descendents of future generations, who we are and how we live our lives will have an impact on them in some way.

Regardless of our age today, there is always something we can do for the benefit of others. What we do may not be on a large scale, and it may not draw public attention, but it can be important all the same. What matters most is that we offer up our resources, however limited; and dedicate our effort, however simple.

Our goal is not to live in such a way that we will be remembered after our death, but to live our moments fully because we will only live them once. All that will matter is that while we were alive, we loved with our whole heart and lived with our whole being.

ADOLFO QUEZADA, a retired counselor and psychotherapist, has authored fifteen books on psycho-spiritual issues. He holds master's degrees in counseling and in journalism from the University of Arizona. Quezada is married and has four children and five grandchildren. He lives in Tucson, Arizona.

Made in the USA
San Bernardino, CA
28 May 2015